TREASURY OF LITERATURE

BLUE WATERS

SENIOR AUTHORS
ROGER C. FARR
DOROTHY S. STRICKLAND

AUTHORS
RICHARD F. ABRAHAMSON
ELLEN BOOTH CHURCH
BARBARA BOWEN COULTER
BERNICE E. CULLINAN
MARGARET A. GALLEGO
W. DORSEY HAMMOND
JUDITH L. IRVIN
KAREN KUTIPER
DONNA M. OGLE
TIMOTHY SHANAHAN
PATRICIA SMITH
JUNKO YOKOTA
HALLIE KAY YOPP

SENIOR CONSULTANTS
ASA G. HILLIARD III
JUDY M. WALLIS

CONSULTANTS
ALONZO A. CRIM
ROLANDO R. HINOJOSA-SMITH
LEE BENNETT HOPKINS
ROBERT J. STERNBERG

HARCOURT BRACE & COMPANY
Orlando Atlanta Austin Boston San Francisco Chicago Dallas New York
Toronto London

8 9 10   032   97 96

Acknowledgments

For permission to reprint copyrighted material, grateful acknowledgment is made to the following sources:

Jose Aruego and Ariane Dewey: Illustrations by Jose Aruego and Ariane Dewey from *Sea Frog, City Frog* by Dorothy O. Van Woerkom. Illustrations copyright © 1985 by Jose Aruego and Ariane Dewey.

Dell, a division of Bantam Doubleday Dell Publishing Group, Inc.: Cover illustration from *My Friend Whale* by Simon James. Copyright © 1990 by Simon James.

Dial Books for Young Readers, a division of Penguin Books USA Inc.: "Vegetables" from *Lionel at Large* by Stephen Krensky, illustrated by Susanna Natti. Text copyright © 1986 by Stephen Krensky; illustrations copyright © 1986 by Susanna Natti.

Dutton Children's Books, a division of Penguin Books USA Inc.: *Punky Goes Fishing* by Sally G. Ward. Copyright © 1991 by Sally G. Ward.

Ediciones Ekaré, Caracas, Venezuela: Cover illustration by Marcela Cabrera from *The Absent-Minded Toad* by Javier Rondón. © 1988 by Ediciones Ekaré. Originally published in Spanish under the title *El Sapo Distraido.*

Green Tiger Press, an imprint of Simon & Schuster, Inc.: Cover illustration by Lisa Etre from *One White Sail* by S.T. Garne. Illustration copyright © 1992 by Lisa Etre.

Greenwillow Books, a division of William Morrow & Company, Inc.: *The Doorbell Rang* by Pat Hutchins. Copyright © 1986 by Pat Hutchins.

HarperCollins Publishers: "Cookies" from *Frog and Toad Together* by Arnold Lobel. Copyright © 1972 by Arnold Lobel. Cover illustration from *Mouse Soup* by Arnold Lobel. Copyright © 1977 by Arnold Lobel. "Little Bear and Owl" from *Father Bear Comes Home* by Else Holmelund Minarik, illustrated by Maurice Sendak. Text copyright © 1959 by Else Holmelund Minarik; illustrations copyright © 1959 by Maurice Sendak.

Henry Holt and Company, Inc.: Cover illustration from *Fish Faces* by Norbert Wu. Copyright © 1993 by Norbert Wu.

Little, Brown and Company: The Cake That Mack Ate by Rose Robart, illustrated by Maryann Kovalski. Text copyright © 1986 by Rose Robart; illustrations copyright © 1986 by Maryann Kovalski.

Little, Brown and Company, in association with Joy Street Books: D.W. All Wet by Marc Brown. Copyright © 1988 by Marc Brown.

Lothrop, Lee & Shepard Books, a division of William Morrow & Company, Inc.: "Seaside" from *Out and About* by Shirley Hughes. Text copyright © 1988 by Shirley Hughes. Cover illustration by Jan Ormerod from *Eat Up, Gemma* by Sarah Hayes. Illustration copyright © 1988 by Jan Ormerod.

Gina Maccoby Literary Agency: From *Nuts To You & Nuts To Me* (Retitled: "Cookie Cutters") by Mary Ann Hoberman. Text copyright © 1974 by Mary Ann Hoberman. Published by Alfred A. Knopf.

Macmillan Publishing Company, a Division of Macmillan, Inc.: Sea Frog, City Frog by Dorothy O. Van Woerkom. Text copyright © 1975 by Dorothy O. Van Woerkom.

N. Van Wright Mellage: "To Catch a Fish" by N. Van Wright Mellage. Text © 1990 by Nanette Van Wright Mellage.

Morrow Junior Books, a division of William Morrow & Company, Inc.: Cover illustration from *Yellow Ball* by Molly Bang. Copyright © 1991 by Molly Bang.

Orchard Books, New York: Cover illustration by David Soman from *When I Am Old with You* by Angela Johnson. Illustration copyright © 1990 by David Soman. Cover illustration by Bill Slavin from *Sitting on the Farm* by Bob King. Illustration copyright © 1991 by Bill Slavin. Originally published in Canada by Kids Can Press Ltd.

Raintree Publishers, a division of Steck-Vaughn Company: From *Peanut Butter, Apple Butter, Cinnamon Toast* by Argentina Palacios, illustrated by Ben Mahan. © 1990 by American Teacher Publications. Published by Steck-Vaughn Company.

Random House, Inc.: "The Fish That Goes Fishing" from *Fish Do the Strangest Things* by Leonora and Arthur Hornblow. Text copyright © 1966 by Random House, Inc.

Elizabeth Roach: "Cookies" from *Rhymes About Us* by Marchette Chute. Text copyright 1974 by Marchette Chute.

Jean Stangl: "Peanut Butter Balls" (Retitled: "Make Peanut Butter Balls") from *The No-Cook Cookery Cookbook* by Jean Stangl. Text copyright © 1976 by Mary Jean Stangl.

Sterling Publishing Co., Inc., 387 Park Ave. S., New York, NY 10016: "A Sailor Went to Sea, Sea, Sea" from *Musical Games for Children of All Ages* by Esther L. Nelson. Text © 1976 by Esther L. Nelson.

Continued on page 204

Dear Reader,

Reading can take you many places. Come and sail on the blue waters. These stories will let you meet new faces. You can learn Native American water signs. You will read a Japanese folktale about two silly frogs. You will meet many different animals and people in this book.

All kinds of people make up a beautiful world. In the same way, all the stories you will read fit together to form a beautiful book. Set sail and get ready!

Sincerely,
The Authors

Unit One
Waterways / 8

Unit Two
Food Fun / 112

U N I T O N E

Waterways

"If all the seas were one sea
what a great sea it would be . . ."
Mother Goose

Being around water is lots of fun.
What do you like to do near water?
Maybe you like to ride in a boat.
Did you know that the Haida
Indians built boats? As you read
these stories, you'll meet others
who like to do things near water.

THEMES

BOOKSHELF

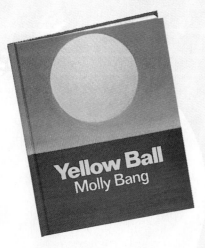

YELLOW BALL
by Molly Bang

A yellow ball is left too close to the water. It floats out to sea. Follow the yellow ball as it travels high and low, above and below, and into a terrible storm.

Award-Winning Author

Harcourt Brace Library Book

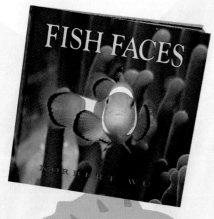

FISH FACES
by Norbert Wu

Meet some "fish that dart up and dip and slide" and "fish with mouths that open wide." You must see these fish to believe them!

Harcourt Brace Library Book

One White Sail

by S. T. Garne

What would you see on a Caribbean island? Sailboats? Palm trees? Steel drums? You will see all these things and more when you read this book!

When I Am Old with You

by Angela Johnson

Do you like to fish and go to the beach? Then come along with a girl and her grandaddy. They have lots of fun together!

ALA Notable Book

My Friend Whale

by Simon James

The boy in this story has a very big friend. It's a whale! You will learn a lot about blue whales when you read this story.

12

THEME

Sand and Sea

Do you like to play in the water?
Read a story and a poem about
fun in the water. Then have fun
with Native American water signs.

CONTENTS

D.W. ALL WET
written and illustrated
by Marc Brown

WATER SIGNS
by Karen Liptak

SEASIDE
by Shirley Hughes

D.W. ALL WET

Marc Brown

AWARD-WINNING
AUTHOR/
ILLUSTRATOR

"It's too hot!" shouted D.W.

"That's why we came to the beach,"
said Mother.

"I don't like the beach," said D.W.

"And I don't like to get wet."

"Here's a good spot," said Father.

"When are we leaving?" asked D.W.

"We just got here," said Mother.

"Come on, D.W. Take off your robe,"
said Arthur.
"Last one in is a rotten egg!"

"I'm not playing," said D.W.

"I don't want to get sunburned.
And no splashing!"

"Come on in," called Arthur. "The water's great!"

"I don't want to," said D.W. "I don't like the water."

"You haven't even tried it," said Father.

"Is it time to go yet?" asked D.W.

"Not yet," said Arthur.
"I'm going for a walk."
"Me, too!" said D.W.
"You walk. I'll ride.
Help me up!"

"But I can't see!" said Arthur.
"You don't need to," said D.W.
"I'll tell you where to go."

"Go!" she said.

"Where are we going?" asked Arthur.

"It's a surprise," said D.W.
"Keep walking. Now turn left.
Arthur, I said left. Turn left!"
cried D.W.
"Not that way! Stop!"

SPLASH!

"Help! Help!" screamed D.W. "I can't swim!"

"You don't have to," said Arthur.
"Just stand up."

Then D.W. dipped,

floated,

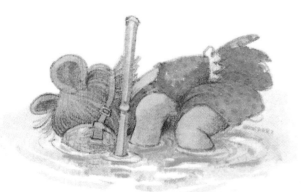

flipped,

flopped,

squirted,

splashed,

and dunked.

"Time to go!" called Father.
"Let's come back tomorrow!" said D.W.

☀ Does D.W. remind you of someone you know?
Tell about that person.

☀ What made D.W. change her mind about the
beach?

WRITE   D.W. wants to tell a friend about her
day at the beach. Write what she will say.

WATER SIGNS

BY KAREN LIPTAK

illustrations by
Scott Scheidly • Ann Morton Hubbard

Make the Indian water signs
that you see in the pictures. Try to
speak to a friend using these signs.

WATER (DRINK)

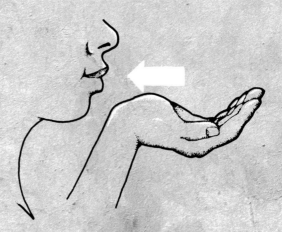

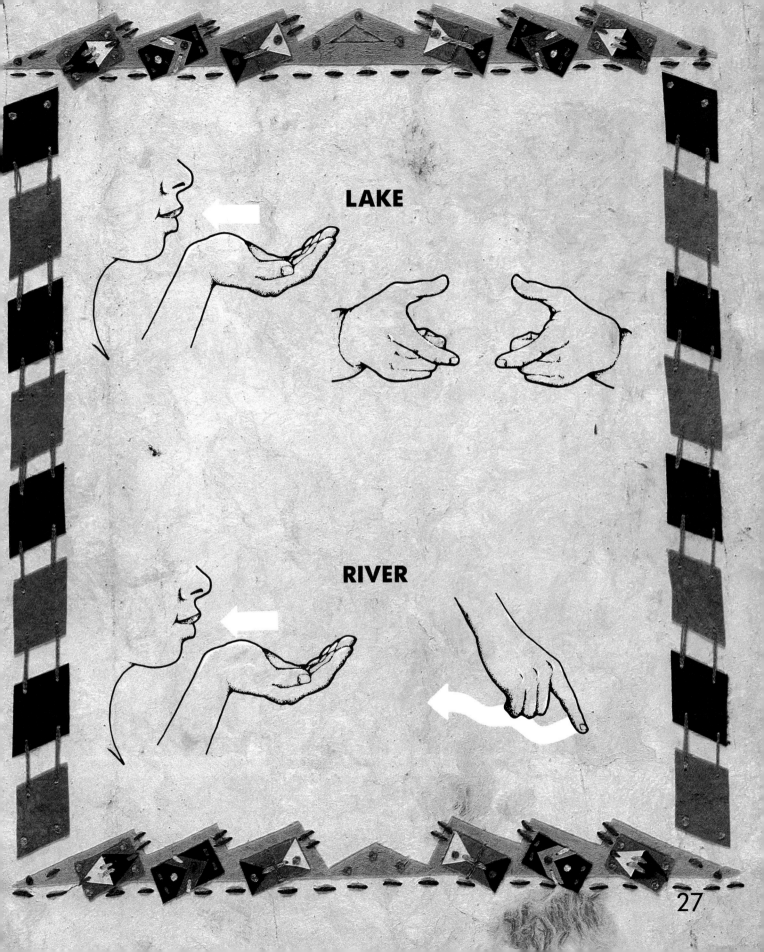

LAKE

RIVER

BOAT

CANOE

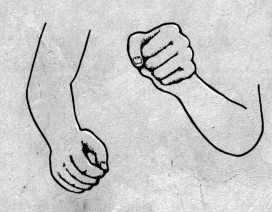

28

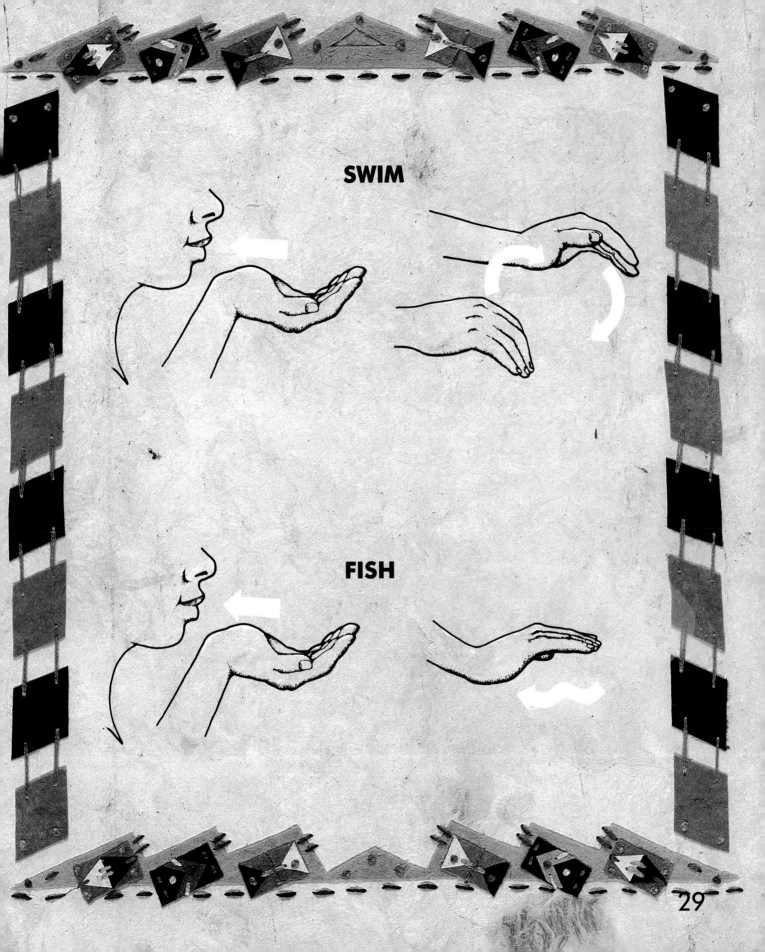

SWIM

FISH

29

SEASIDE

Sand in the sandwiches,
Sand in the tea,
Flat, wet sand running
Down to the sea.
Pools full of seaweed,
Shells and stones,
Damp bathing suits
And ice-cream cones.

Waves pouring in
To a sand-castle moat.
Mend the defenses!
Now we're afloat!
Water's for splashing,
Sand is for play,
A day by the sea
Is the best kind of day.

Shirley Hughes

Edward Henry Potthast
1857–1927
Children on the Beach
Hirshhorn Collection

Sand and Sea

What words would you use to tell about a day at the beach?

If you could spend a day at the beach, what would you do?

WRITER'S WORKSHOP

Write a story about what you might do or see in the water. Tell what you would do first, next, and last.

T H E M E

Visit Me

Who do you like to visit? Read some stories about a girl and some frogs who go visiting. Then sing a sailor song.

C O N T E N T S

33

JENNY'S JOURNEY

SHEILA WHITE SAMTON

One day Jenny got a letter
from her best friend,
who had moved far away.
Jenny felt sad because
her friend was lonely.

35

Jenny wrote back right away:

Here I come!

The sun is rising and

I'm setting out!

I'm sailing my boat

through the tugboats and the sailboats

and the motorboats and the ferries,

"Where are you going?"

and past the statue of
Our Lady of the Harbor,

and under a bridge,

till I get to the open sea!

Maria, I wake up all alone on the ocean!

Remember how lonely I felt when you

moved away?

I feel lonely now, too, but then

a dolphin shoots out of the water.

Then another one!

And here come

some sea gulls!

They all want my breakfast!

It's like the day we fed the seals at the zoo.

45

"Little girl, little girl,
where are you going?"

"Don't worry,
don't worry.
I'm going to
visit Maria."

I sail along. Suddenly I'm in
the shadow of a big, black wall!

It's an ocean liner! Far above
my head, a voice booms out.

That night I steer my boat

through a chain of islands.

When I open my eyes
in the morning, *Oh, no!*
I'm caught in a storm at sea!
The howling wind fills my sail,
and all day long,
I steer up and down
waves like mountains,

"Oh, Maria, don't you cry for me,

for I'm comin' for to see ya,

right across the deep blue sea."

until the ocean is calm again,

and I can take out my guitar and sing.

By now you probably think I'll never
get there. But the next day,

I finally see land!

There's a long pier

and *you* are on it,

waiting for me!

Hooray!

So don't feel lonely.
(And someday I really
will come to see you!)

Love, your friend,

Jenny

- How did you feel at the end of the story?

- How do you know that Jenny's journey was a make-believe journey?

WRITE   Maria wants to write a letter to Jenny.
Write what she might say in her letter.

Sea Frog, City Frog

A JAPANESE FOLKTALE
BY DOROTHY O. VAN WOERKOM
ILLUSTRATED BY JOSE ARUEGO AND ARIANE DEWEY

Sea Frog,
City Frog
BY DOROTHY O. VAN WOERKOM
PICTURES BY JOSE ARUEGO & ARIANE DEWEY

Sea Frog lived in a bog by the sea.
City Frog lived in a pond in the city.
One day when the sun was bright,
Sea Frog said, "How nice it would be
to see the city!"
And City Frog said, "I would
like to see the sea!"

So City Frog jumped
out of his pond.
He hopped
down the road
to the sea.

And Sea Frog jumped
out of his bog.
He hopped up the road
to the city.

The two frogs
hopped for a day
and a night.
At last they came
to a hill.

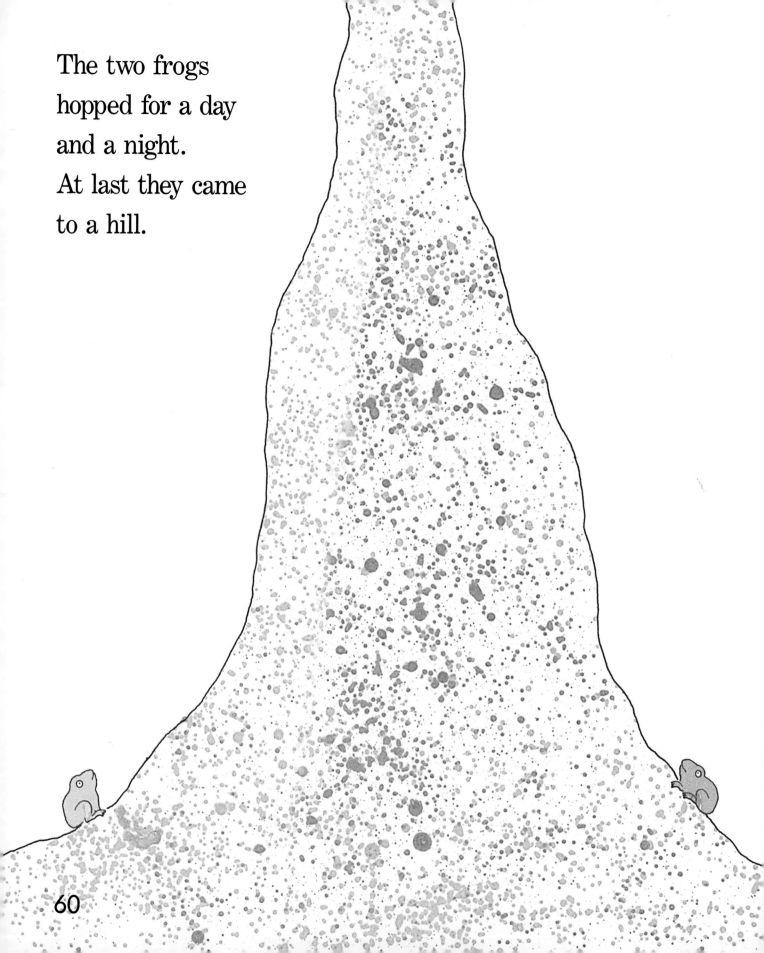

60

Up one side
of the hill
hopped City Frog.
How tired he was!

Up the other side
of the hill
hopped Sea Frog.
And he was tired!

61

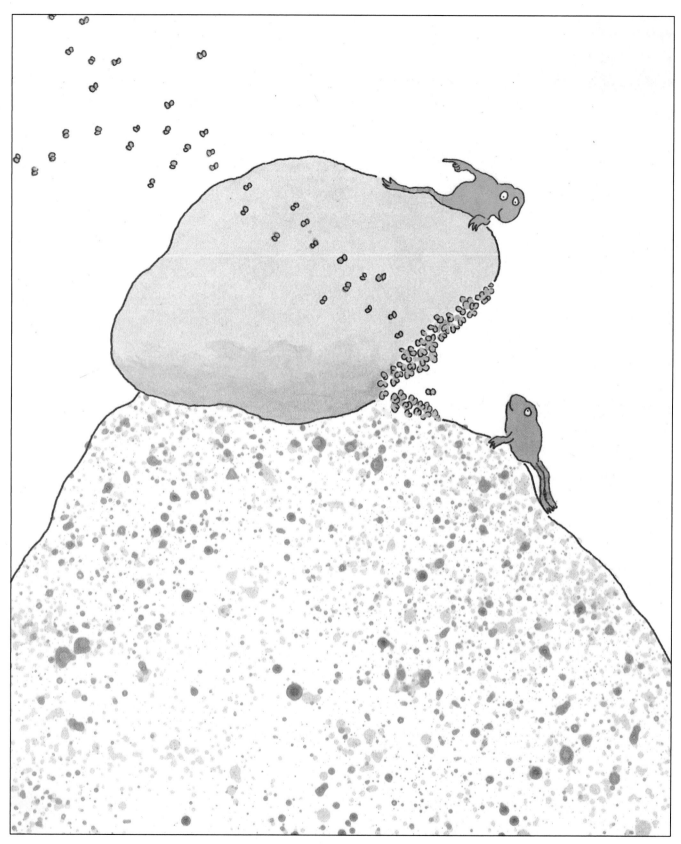

The two frogs met
at the top of the hill.
"Hello!" said City Frog.
"I am from the city.
I am going to the sea.
Where are you from?
Where are you going?"
Sea Frog said,
"I am from the sea,
and I am going to the city."
"How nice that we should meet,"
said City Frog.
"Let us rest and talk for an hour."

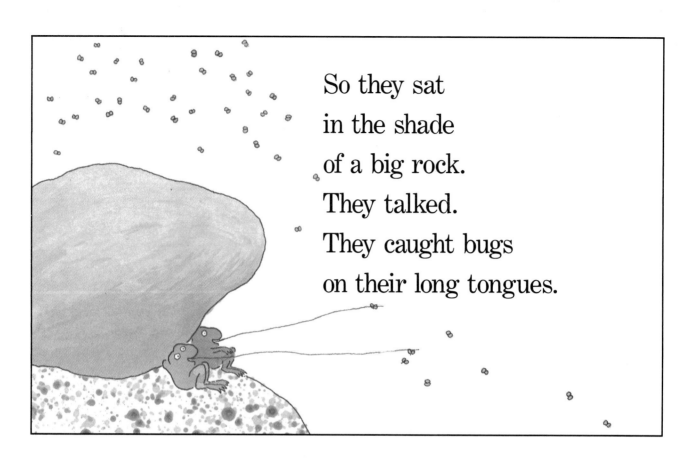

So they sat
in the shade
of a big rock.
They talked.
They caught bugs
on their long tongues.

They even took a nap.
Then City Frog woke up.
"I wish," he said,
"that we were tall."
Sea Frog opened one eye.
"What good would that do?"
he said.

"Would it get you
to the sea, and me
to the city?"
"No," said City Frog.
"But here we are
on top of this hill.
Now, if we were tall,
we could see far away."
"How smart you are!"
Sea Frog said.
"And we can do it!
We can make ourselves tall."

65

"Show me how we can do that,"
said City Frog.
"Like this," said Sea Frog.
Sea Frog stood up with his
front legs in the air.
"We can make ourselves tall
if we hold onto each other!"
So the frogs stood up on their
long hind legs.
With their short front legs
they held onto each other.

"I can see a long way!"
said City Frog.
"So can I," Sea Frog said.

So City Frog turned his nose
to the sea.
And Sea Frog turned his nose
to the city.
The poor, silly frogs!
Their noses were turned
where they wanted to go.
But their great eyes—which were
at the back of their heads—
only saw where they had been!

"Oh, my!" said Sea Frog.
"The city is just like the sea!"

"Dear me!" said City Frog.
"The sea is just like the city!"

So the frogs went home again. And they never knew
that the sea is not at all like the city, and the city
is not at all like the sea.

🐚 How did you feel when the frogs went back to
their homes?

🐚 Why didn't the frogs finish their journeys?

WRITE   Tell Sea Frog about the city. Or, tell
City Frog about the sea. Write what you would say.

70

Jose Aruego
and
Ariane Dewey

Jose Aruego and Ariane Dewey made the pictures for Sea Frog, City Frog.

Jose Aruego grew up in the Philippines. His family had birds, dogs, cats, chickens, roosters, pigs, ducks, and horses. This may be why Mr. Aruego loves to draw animals. He says his animals' funny faces often make him laugh while he works.

Ariane Dewey was born in Chicago, Illinois. When she was in the fourth grade, she wrote a book and drew the pictures. It was then that she knew she wanted to become a painter. Ms. Dewey loves color. She adds the colors to Jose Aruego's pictures.

Because Ariane Dewey likes to paint and Jose Aruego likes to draw, they work very well together.

71

A Sailor Went to Sea, Sea, Sea

by Esther L. Nelson

A sailor went to sea, sea, sea,
To see what he could see, see, see, but
All that he could see, see, see,
Was the bottom of the deep blue
sea, sea, sea.

Visit Me

Imagine that Jenny and the frogs
want to go on a trip together.
Where would they go?

Could these stories really
happen? Tell why or why not.

WRITER'S WORKSHOP

Think of a time you went to visit
someone. Write a poem about
your visit.

T H E M E

Going Fishing

Would you like to go fishing?
Read about fishing and some fish
that were caught!

C O N T E N T S

75

Punky Goes Fishing

by SALLY G. WARD

Punky was sleeping over at her grandparents'
house.

"Grampy," she asked, "may I go fishing
with you tomorrow?"

"Well, Punky," said Grampy, "let me think
about it. Fishing is serious business, you know."

The next morning, Punky had just finished
her breakfast when Grampy surprised her.
"What do you say, Punky . . . want to try
some fishing?"
So they prepared their lunches, and Punky
put on her old clothes.
"I'm bringing a towel, in case you get
wet," said Grampy.

Grampy gave Punky a little fishing pole.
"It's just the right size for you, Punky,"
he said. "And here's
my great big one for
catching the big fish."

"I want you to wear this life jacket, dear,
so Grampy knows you're safe."
"Don't you need to
wear one, Grampy?"
asked Punky.
"Oh no,"
Grampy laughed.
"I never fall in."

Out on the water, Punky watched the houses
get smaller.

"It's so quiet out here, Grampy," she said.

"That's why I like it," Grampy replied.

"And here's where we stop, Punky."

"The water is only up to my middle.
Plenty safe. I'll set the anchor."
The anchor went in easily.
But so did Grampy's lunch.

"That's all right, Grampy. You can
share mine."
"Thank you, Punky," said Grampy.
Grampy got the poles ready,
and they sat back to wait.

"Any nibbles yet, Grampy?"

"Nope . . . well, wait a minute. . . ."

"Wow, Grampy. You caught a teeny one."

"Yup," he said, "that one goes right back in."

The fish went in easily.
But so did one of the oars.
"Good thing I brought my waders," said
Grampy. "When we're done, I'll *pull* us
back to shore."

84

"I'm hungry, Grampy. Let's have lunch."
"Good idea, Punky. I'm hungry, too."

After lunch Grampy said, "Let's try one
more time, all right?"
"Sure," said Punky. "Only, can I fix
my own hook? I want to try a little piece
of the leftover fig bar on it."

"Ha ha," laughed Grampy. "Never heard of
a fish who wanted to take a bite of a fig bar."

"Take it from me. Your old grandpa knows what's what. Especially when it comes to fishing."

"Grampy! I think I've got something!
GRAMPY! I *know* I've got something!"
"Keep reeling, Punky. I'm coming.
Looks like a whopper! GOTCHA!"

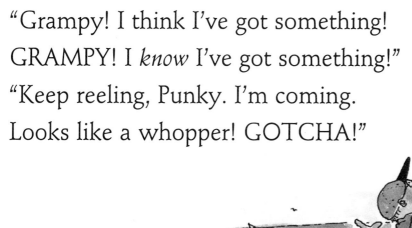

The fish stayed in the net.
But Grampy went over.

"Wow, Grampy!
Wait till Grammy sees
what I caught."

It was time to go home.

"Grampy! You got a fish, too!
Can we go again tomorrow?"

▨ Would you like to go fishing with Grampy?
Why or why not?

▨ How do you know that Punky had fun fishing
with Grampy?

WRITE   Imagine that you are Punky. Write a letter
to your family. Tell them about your fishing trip.

THE FISH THAT GOES FISHING

by Leonora and Arthur Hornblow

People catch many strange fish.
But one of the strangest fish of all
does her own fishing.
She lives down deep in the dark sea.
She is called the deep-sea angler.
The deep-sea angler has
her own fishing rod.
It grows out of the top of
her head and hangs in
front of her mouth.
The tip of her rod shines in
the deep dark water.

This tip is the bait on her fishing rod. Hungry fish see her bait. They think it is something to eat. A hungry fish will swim toward the shiny bait.

The angler opens her wide mouth.
The fish swims closer and closer.
He swims right at the bait. Then the
angler closes her mouth. Snap!
That's the end of that fish.

illustrated by Bernie Knox

TO CATCH A FISH

Dana went to catch a fish
He took his fishing pole
And cast his line into the lake
A chocolate cookie was his bait
He sat upon a rock to wait
To catch a great big fish

Suddenly he heard Blub Blub
Two fish stuck out their heads
"Offer us our favorite dishes
Worms or flies or smaller fishes
Maybe then you'll get your wish"
And off they swam, Blub Blub!

Nanette Mellage
illustrated by Floyd Cooper

FATHER BEAR COMES HOME

by ELSE HOLMELUND MINARIK

pictures by MAURICE SENDAK
by the author and artist of LITTLE BEAR

HARPER TROPHY

ALA
NOTABLE
BOOK

An I CAN READ Book®

LITTLE BEAR AND OWL

"Little Bear," said Mother Bear,

"can you be my fisherman?"

"Yes, I can," said Little Bear.

"Good," said Mother Bear.

"Will you go down to the river?

Will you catch a fish for us?"

"Yes, I will," said Little Bear.

So Little Bear went down

to the river.

And there he saw Owl.

Owl was sitting on a log.

"Hello, Little Bear," said Owl.

"Hello, Owl," said Little Bear.

"Father Bear is not home.

He is fishing on the ocean.

But Mother Bear wants a fish now,

so I have to catch one."

"Good," said Owl.

"Catch one."

Little Bear fished.

"I have one," he said.

"Is it too little?"

"It looks good to me," said Owl.

"Well," said Little Bear,

"Father Bear can catch big fish.

He sails in a big boat, too."

Owl said,

"Someday you will be a big bear.

You will catch big fish.

And you will sail in a boat,

like Father Bear."

"I know what," said Little Bear.

"We can make believe.

The log can be a boat.

I will be Father Bear.

You can be you, and we are fishing."

"Where are we fishing?" asked Owl.

"On the ocean," said Little Bear.

"All right," said Owl.

"Hurray!" said Little Bear.

"See what I have."

"What is it?" asked Owl.

"An octopus," said Little Bear.

"Oh," said Owl.

"But see what I have."

"What is it?" asked Little Bear.

"A whale," said Owl.

"But a whale is too big,"
said Little Bear.

"This is a little whale," said Owl.

Just then Mother Bear came along.

"Where is the fish?" she asked.

Little Bear laughed. He said,

"How about an octopus?"

"An octopus!" said Mother Bear.

"Well, then," said Owl,

"how about a little whale?"

"A WHALE!!" said Mother Bear.

"No, thank you. No whale."

"Then how about this fish?"
said Little Bear.

"Yes, thank you," said Mother Bear,

"that is just what I want."

Little Bear said, "You will see.

When I am as big as Father Bear,

I will catch a real octopus."

"Yes, and sail in a real boat,"

said Owl.

"I know it," said Mother Bear.

Owl said, "Little Bear fishes very well."

"Oh, yes," said Mother Bear,
"he fishes very well, indeed.
He is a real fisherman,
just like his father."

What did you like best about Little Bear?

How can you tell that Little Bear wants to be like Father Bear?

WRITE What did Little Bear and Owl pretend to do? What else could they pretend? Write your idea.

Going Fishing

If you went fishing with Punky and Grampy, what would you tell them?

Which fish would you like to catch, Punky's fish or Little Bear's fish?

WRITER'S WORKSHOP

Imagine that you go fishing with your classmates. What do you see, smell, and hear? Write about it.

CONNECTIONS

Multicultural Connection

Beautiful Boats

Long ago, the Haida Indians made big, beautiful boats. Building them was hard work. The Haida carved pictures on their boats. They painted beautiful paintings on their boats, too. Even the oars were carved and painted.

Draw a boat.
Draw or paint beautiful pictures on your boat.

Social Studies Connection

All Kinds of Boats

Boats are used in many different ways. Go to the library. Find pictures of two kinds of boats. How are the boats like those made by the Haida? How are they different? Make a report to show what you have learned.

Science Connection

Float or Sink

Why do you think boats float instead of sinking? What are some other things that float? What are some things that sink? Put some things in water to see what happens. Make a list of things that sink and things that float.

UNIT TWO
2
Food Fun

What foods do you like? Do you know how to cook? You will learn how to make peanut butter balls. Then meet a man who made more than 300 things using peanuts! His name is George Washington Carver. As you read, think about all the fun you can have with food.

THEMES

BOOKSHELF

EAT UP, GEMMA

by Sarah Hayes

Everyone says "Eat up, Gemma." But Gemma is a baby who does not want to eat. Gemma's brother thinks of a good idea to get Gemma to "eat up."

Harcourt Brace Library Book

SITTING ON THE FARM

by Bob King

"Hey, Bug, get off my knee," says a girl. "No siree!" shouts the bug. What will the girl do now? This silly story will really make you laugh!

Harcourt Brace Library Book

114

Not Yet, Yvette

by Helen Ketteman

"Is it time yet, Dad?" asks Yvette again and again. "Not yet, Yvette," answers her father. What is Yvette waiting for? Why is it so hard to wait?

Mouse Soup

by Arnold Lobel

"Ah!" said the weasel. "I am going to make mouse soup." "Oh!" said the mouse. "I am going to *be* mouse soup." Will the mouse become mouse soup?

Children's Choice

The Absent-Minded Toad

by Javier Rondón

The absent-minded toad enjoys his trip to the market. There is so much to see there! When he gets back home—oh, my!

Award-Winning Author

What's Cooking?

Do you help cook meals? You can
read about how a cake is made.
Then you can make your own treat.

CONTENTS

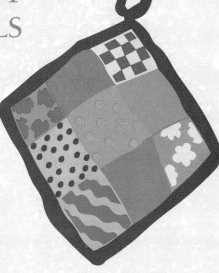

This is the cake that Mack ate.

This is the egg
That went into the cake
that Mack ate.

This is the hen
That laid the egg,
That went into the cake
that Mack ate.

This is the corn
That fed the hen,
That laid the egg,
That went into the cake
  that Mack ate.

This is the seed
That grew into corn,
That fed the hen,
That laid the egg,
That went into the cake
   that Mack ate.

This is the farmer
Who planted the seed,
That grew into corn,
That fed the hen,
That laid the egg,
That went into the cake
that Mack ate.

This is the woman
Who married the farmer,
Who planted the seed,
That grew into corn,
That fed the hen,
That laid the egg,
That went into the cake
that Mack ate.

These are the candles
That lit up the cake,
That was made by the woman,
Who married the farmer,
Who planted the seed,
That grew into corn,
That fed the hen,
That laid the egg,
That went into the cake
    that Mack ate.

This is Mack . . .

He ate the cake.

🍰 How did you feel when Mack ate the cake?

🍰 Name the things that went into the cake that Mack ate.

WRITE   Now a new cake needs to be made. You will be the baker. Write a list of things that you will put in the cake. Draw a picture of your cake.

MAKE PEANUT BUTTER BALLS
BY JEAN STANGL

Mack ate the cake. Now you can make and eat a tasty treat, too!

powdered sugar

powdered milk

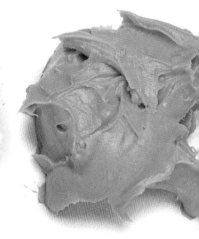

peanut butter

❶ Put 2 tablespoons of powdered sugar in a bowl.

❷ Add 2 tablespoons of powdered milk.

❸ Add 4 tablespoons of peanut butter and stir.

graham crackers

EQUIPMENT
Gather the things you will need.

plastic bag   bowl

rolling pin

spoon   tablespoon

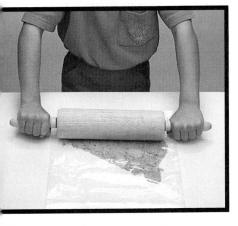

❹ Crush 3 graham crackers in a bag.

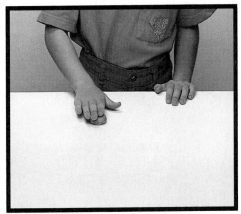

❺ Roll the dough into balls.

❻ Roll the balls in the graham cracker crumbs.

Enjoy your peanut butter balls.

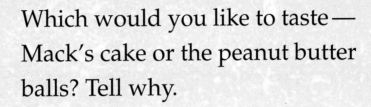

What's Cooking?

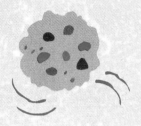

Which would you like to taste—
Mack's cake or the peanut butter
balls? Tell why.

Which of the things you read
about would you most like to
cook? Why?

WRITER'S WORKSHOP

Imagine that you have baked
something. Would Mack eat it?
Write a story about it.

135

THEME

What Are You Eating?

Do you have a favorite food?
Read about some favorite—and
some not so favorite—foods!

CONTENTS

VEGETABLES

Lionel and his family were eating dinner. They were having hamburgers. Lionel liked to eat around the edge of his roll before biting into the middle. The middle was covered with ketchup. "Wipe your face, Lionel," said Mother. "It's covered with ketchup."

Lionel used his napkin.

"What about Louise?" he asked.

His big sister smiled at him.

"My face is clean," said Louise.

"I never make a mess at the table."

She carefully ate a green bean.

It was her last one.

Lionel's plate was still full

of green beans.

He stared at them.

"Eat your vegetables, Lionel," said Father.

His father always ate everything.

"There's no room for them,"
said Lionel.

"You had room for your hamburger,"
said Mother.

She always ate everything too.

"That was different," said Lionel.

"Oh?" said Mother.

Lionel looked down at his stomach.

"I have shelves in here," he explained.

"They hold the food I eat."

Lionel felt one rib.

"Here is my hamburger shelf," he said.

Lionel felt another rib.

"Here is my bread shelf," he said.

"What about your vegetable shelf?" asked Father.

Lionel felt both sides.

"I don't have one," he said.

"Hmmmph!" said Louise.

"If Lionel says he doesn't have a
vegetable shelf," said Father,
"I believe him."

"So do I," said Mother. "And we can't
expect him to eat his vegetables if he
has no place to put them."

Lionel smiled.

"Time for dessert," said Mother.

"Hooray!" said Lionel.

"Too bad you can't have any, Lionel,"
said Father.

"What do you mean?" Lionel asked.

"I've read a lot about these shelves,"
said Father. "The books say that
if you have no vegetable shelf, you have
no dessert shelf either."

"Hooray," said Louise. "Now there will
be more for me."

Lionel felt his ribs again.

"Wait!" he shouted. "I think
I found my vegetable shelf.
It was hidden under the bread shelf."

He began eating his beans.

"See," he said. "I was right."

"How lucky," said Father.

"That was a close call," said Mother.

Lionel thought so too.

🌸 How did you feel when Lionel had to eat his green beans?

🌸 Why did Lionel say he had shelves in his stomach?

WRITE Write a list of foods that you don't like. Write a list of foods that you like very much.

In My Mother's House

BY ANN NOLAN CLARK

ALA
AWARD

Red chili and meat and melons
and yellow cornmeal
I have to eat.

Apricots and peaches
And little red plums
I have to eat.

Big round tortillas
And brown frijoles
I have to eat.
I eat them;
I like them.

ILLUSTRATED BY VELINO HERRERA

Peanut Butter, Apple Butter, Cinnamon Toast

by Argentina Palacios
pictures by Ben Mahan

Peanut butter, apple butter,
cinnamon toast.
What are the foods we like
the most?
Peanut butter, apple butter,
gingerbread man.
Guess our riddles if you can.

148

Red sauce on white noodles.

Grate on lots of cheese.

Don't you want that meatball?

Pass it to me, please.

What is it?

Spaghetti

It's fluffy, white, and crunchy—
A perfect movie treat.
You pop it in a popper,
Then scoop some up to eat.
What is it?

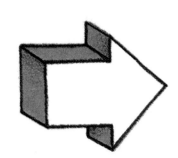

Popcorn

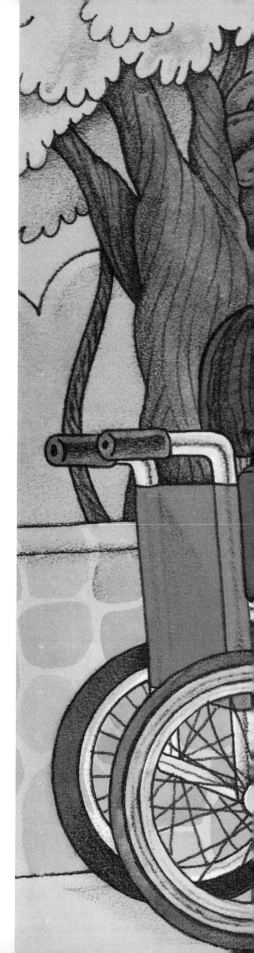

This fruit is long and yellow,
A monkey's favorite meal.
You can eat one anytime,
But first take off the peel.
What is it?

153

A banana

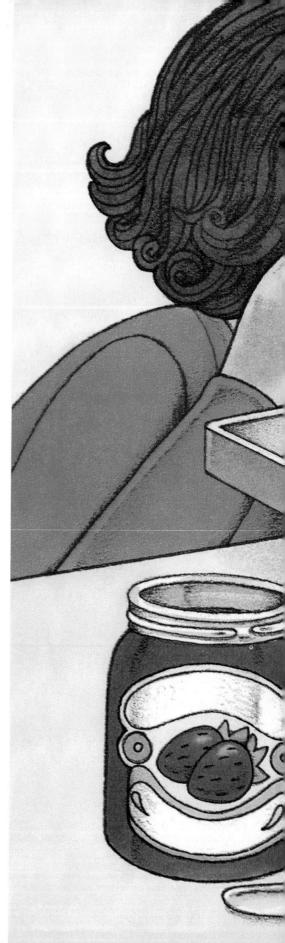

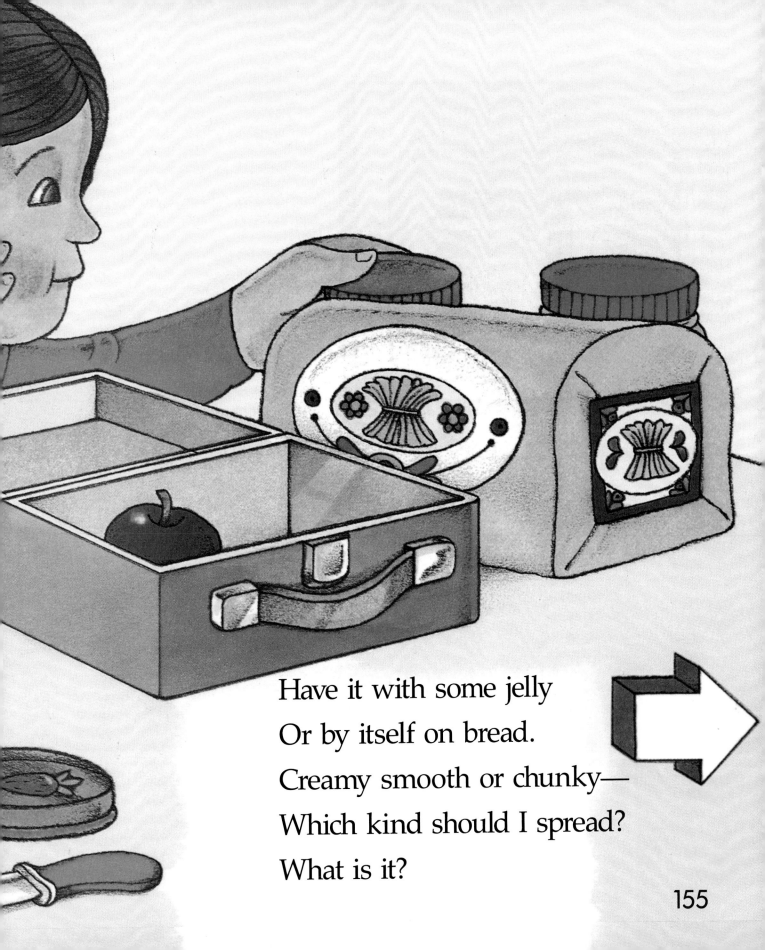

Have it with some jelly
Or by itself on bread.
Creamy smooth or chunky—
Which kind should I spread?
What is it?

Peanut butter

Peanut butter, apple butter, cinnamon toast.
What are the foods YOU like the most?

157

Words About the Author:
Argentina Palacios

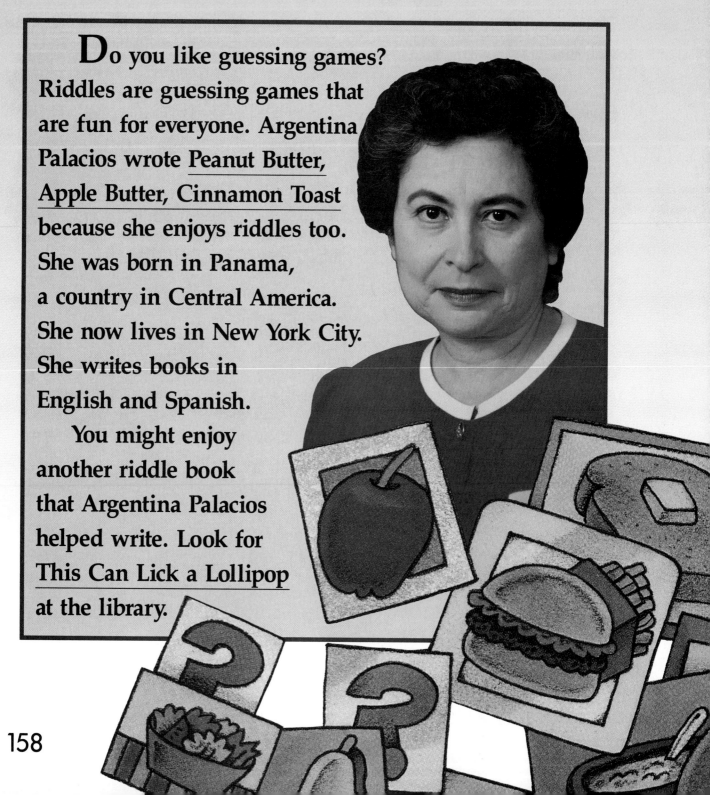

Do you like guessing games? Riddles are guessing games that are fun for everyone. Argentina Palacios wrote <u>Peanut Butter, Apple Butter, Cinnamon Toast</u> because she enjoys riddles too. She was born in Panama, a country in Central America. She now lives in New York City. She writes books in English and Spanish.

You might enjoy another riddle book that Argentina Palacios helped write. Look for <u>This Can Lick a Lollipop</u> at the library.

What Are You Eating?

Which foods from the riddles do you think Lionel would like? Why?

Which food shelves would you use for the foods in "Peanut Butter, Apple Butter, Cinnamon Toast"?

WRITER'S WORKSHOP

Write a riddle about a food Lionel likes, a food he doesn't like, or a food YOU like.

THEME

More Cookies, Please

Reading about cookies might be yummy! Here are some stories and poems to share.

CONTENTS

161

Frog and Toad Together

READING RAINBOW Book

ALA NOTABLE BOOK
CHILDREN'S CHOICE

by Arnold Lobel

I CAN READ

Cookies

Toad baked some cookies.
"These cookies smell very good,"
said Toad.
He ate one.
"And they taste even better," he said.
Toad ran to Frog's house.

"Frog, Frog," cried Toad,
"taste these cookies
that I have made."
Frog ate one of the cookies.
"These are the best cookies
I have ever eaten!" said Frog.

Frog and Toad ate many cookies,
one after another.
"You know, Toad," said Frog,
with his mouth full,
"I think we should stop eating.
We will soon be sick."

"You are right," said Toad.
"Let us eat one last cookie,
and then we will stop."
Frog and Toad ate
one last cookie.
There were many cookies
left in the bowl.
"Frog," said Toad,
"let us eat one very last cookie,
and then we will stop."
Frog and Toad
ate one very last cookie.

"We must stop eating!" cried Toad
as he ate another.
"Yes," said Frog,
reaching for a cookie,
"we need will power."
"What is will power?" asked Toad.

"Will power is trying hard
not to do something
that you really want to do,"
said Frog.
"You mean like trying *not* to eat all
of these cookies?" asked Toad.
"Right," said Frog.

Frog put the cookies in a box.
"There," he said.
"Now we will not eat
any more cookies."
"But we can open the box,"
said Toad.
"That is true," said Frog.

Frog tied some string
around the box.
"There," he said.
"Now we will not eat
any more cookies."
"But we can cut the string
and open the box," said Toad.
"That is true," said Frog.

Frog got a ladder.

He put the box up on a high shelf.

"There," said Frog.

"Now we will not eat
any more cookies."

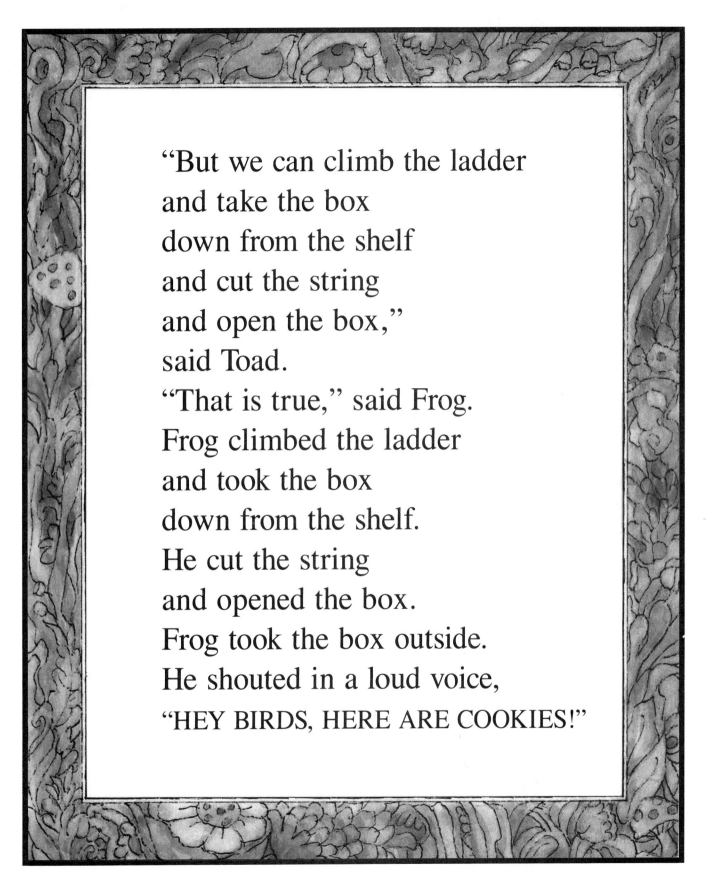

"But we can climb the ladder
and take the box
down from the shelf
and cut the string
and open the box,"
said Toad.
"That is true," said Frog.
Frog climbed the ladder
and took the box
down from the shelf.
He cut the string
and opened the box.
Frog took the box outside.
He shouted in a loud voice,
"HEY BIRDS, HERE ARE COOKIES!"

Birds came from everywhere.
They picked up all the cookies
in their beaks and flew away.
"Now we have no more cookies to eat,"
said Toad sadly.
"Not even one."
"Yes," said Frog, "but we have
lots and lots of will power."
"You may keep it all, Frog," said Toad.
"I am going home now to bake a cake."

✸ How would you have helped Frog and Toad with their problem?

✸ Do you think Frog and Toad have will power? Explain your answer.

WRITE   Add to the story. Write about what you think Frog and Toad will do with the cake.

COOKIES

by Marchette Chute

If I had a kitchen
      And knew how to bake,
These are the cookies
      I would make:
Chocolate, peanut,
      Lemon and spice—
All the ones
      That are extra nice.
And to everyone on the block I'd say,
"Here are the cookies I made today.
Come and eat them right away."

illustrated by Kid Kane

COOKIE CUTTERS

by Mary Ann Hoberman

AWARD-WINNING POET

Cookie cutters
Cutting cookies
Cutting different
Shapes and sizes
First you make them
Next you bake them
Then you take them
And you cool them
And . . .
That's weird.
They've disappeared!

The Doorbell Rang
by Pat Hutchins

"I've made some cookies for tea," said Ma.

"Good," said Victoria and Sam. "We're starving."

"Share them between yourselves," said Ma.

"I made plenty."

"That's six each," said Sam and Victoria.

"They look as good as Grandma's," said Victoria.

"They smell as good as Grandma's," said Sam.

"No one makes cookies like Grandma,"
said Ma as the doorbell rang.
It was Tom and Hannah from next door.
"Come in," said Ma.
"You can share the cookies."

"That's three each," said Sam and Victoria.

"They smell as good as your Grandma's," said Tom.

"And look as good," said Hannah.

"No one makes cookies like Grandma,"
said Ma as the doorbell rang.
It was Peter and his little brother.
"Come in," said Ma.
"You can share the cookies."

"That's two each," said Victoria and Sam.
"They look as good as your Grandma's,"
said Peter. "And smell as good."

"Nobody makes cookies like Grandma,"
said Ma as the doorbell rang.
It was Joy and Simon
with their four cousins.
"Come in," said Ma.
"You can share the cookies."

"That's one each," said Sam and Victoria.

"They smell as good as your Grandma's," said Joy.

"And look as good," said Simon.

"No one makes cookies like Grandma,"
said Ma as the doorbell rang

and rang.

187

"Oh dear," said Ma as the children stared
at the cookies on their plates.

"Perhaps you'd better eat them
before we open the door."
"We'll wait," said Sam.

It was Grandma with an
enormous tray of cookies.

"How nice to have so many friends
to share them with," said Grandma.
"It's a good thing I made a lot!"
"And no one makes cookies like Grandma,"
said Ma as the doorbell rang.

✴ What did you like best about this story?

✴ Were the children good at sharing? How do you know?

WRITE Imagine that you are eating one of Grandma's cookies. Write about how the cookie looks, smells, and tastes.

More Cookies, Please

How could the children from "The Doorbell Rang" help Frog and Toad?

What do you think Frog and Toad would do if Ma and the children rang their doorbell?

WRITER'S WORKSHOP

Which story did you like the best? Write a report. Tell about the story.

CONNECTIONS

Multicultural Connection

George Washington Carver

Do you like soup? Bread? Ice cream? Did you know that these foods can be made from peanuts? It's true! George Washington Carver learned that peanuts can be used to make many things.

Dr. Carver was a great teacher and scientist. He spent his whole life helping others.

Write a sentence telling how you help others. Draw a picture to go with it.

Social Studies Connection

Community Helpers

Name some people who help others. What do they do to help? Imagine that you are a community helper. Act out what you do to help. Ask your classmates to guess who you are.

Math Connection

Peanut Problems

Peanuts grow in shells. Most shells hold two peanuts. Imagine that you open three peanut shells. How many peanuts will you find? Write your own peanut problem. Have a classmate find the answer.

GLOSSARY

A

about	Let's talk **about** our trip to the park.
after	I brush my teeth **after** I eat.
along	Come **along** with us to the beach.
always	The baby **always** takes a nap after lunch.
any	I don't have **any** wings, but a bird does.
around	The grass grew all **around** the pond.
ate	Lee was hungry, so he **ate** some grapes.

after

around

B

beach	At the **beach** we play in the sand and swim.
been	We have **been** to the zoo five times.
before	The sun comes up **before** I wake up.
better	I can throw **better** than I can catch.
biting	The cat is **biting** into the cheese.
boat	It is fun to ride in a **boat** on the lake.
bright	It is very **bright** with all the lights on.

beach

C

cake   We will eat all the **cake.**

children   Dad read a story to the **children.**

climbed   The cat **climbed** up the tree.

cry   The baby began to **cry.**

children

D

dear   Kim said, "Oh, **dear!**" when she saw the mess.

doesn't   A cat **doesn't** have wings, but a bird does.

door   Chen came to our **door** and rang the bell.

door

E

each   Rosa and Mike waved to **each** other.

egg   Dad cooked an **egg** for me.

ever   That is the best bike I have **ever** seen.

egg

F

felt   We **felt** very happy.

flew   The bird **flew** to the tree.

flipped   She **flipped** her feet up and down in the water.

food   Eating **food** helps you grow.

front   The dog dug a hole with its **front** paws.

front

G

girl   We have a new **girl** in our class.

goes   My mom **goes** to work each day.

grew   The little puppy **grew** into a big dog.

H

has   Pat **has** a horse.

having   We are **having** milk with dinner.

held   Dad picked up the baby and **held** her close.

hold   Let's **hold** hands as we cross the street.

held

I

I've   **I've** been playing with my friends.

I've

J

just   We **just** missed the bus.

K

keep   **Keep** on walking fast.

knows   Jerome **knows** how to swim.

L

laid   The hen **laid** eggs in her nest.

last   The boy at the end of the line was **last.**

laughed   I **laughed** at the funny pigs.

laughed

laid

M

made   Gina **made** a hat out of paper.

many   **Many** boys and girls go to our school.

may   **May** I go out to play?

made

N

need   I **need** some water.

next   Tom was **next** in line.

nice   We had a **nice** time at the zoo.

night   Anna goes to sleep at **night.**

nobody   The school was closed, and **nobody** was there.

night

O

oh   **Oh,** this kitten is so soft!

only   There was **only** one peach left.

open   Please **open** the door.

only

P

perhaps   **Perhaps** we can play outside today.

planted   We **planted** the seeds by the tree.

R

rang   When the bell **rang,** it was time to eat.

real   I saw a **real** bear at the zoo.

river   Fish live in the **river.**

real

S

safe   You are **safe** when you use a seat belt.

sail   We will **sail** the boat on the lake.

shadow   My **shadow** and I are always together.

shelf   Nathan put the book on the **shelf.**

should   We **should** clean up this mess.

side   Carmen rode her sled down the **side** of the hill.

shelf

some   There are **some** ducks on the lake.

someday   **Someday** you will have a job.

something   Smiling is **something** you do when you are happy.

spot   We picked a **spot** on the grass and sat down.

stand   Peter sat down, but Ann told him to **stand** up.

stop   **Stop** and look both ways before you cross the street.

stop

201

T

that   I want to eat **that** cake.

their   The girls clap **their** hands.

these   **These** books are mine, and those are yours.

think   I **think** I know where my hat is.

three   My **three** friends are Jan, Taro, and Tonya.

two   I have **two** hands and **two** feet.

three

V

visit   Come and **visit** me soon.

W

water

wait   I had to **wait** for the school bus.

want   I **want** to see my friends today.

water   The **water** in the tub was hot.

way   The **way** to school is down this street.

were   We **were** playing outside.

we're   They want Jan and me to play, so **we're** going now.

whale   A **whale** is the biggest animal in the sea.

whale

woman   Mrs. Jones is a nice **woman.**

wrote   James **wrote** a long letter.

Y

you're   We are glad **you're** here to play.

yourselves   You boys will have to play by **yourselves.**

Acknowledgments continued

Viking Penguin, a division of Penguin Books USA Inc.: From *In My Mother's House* by Ann Nolan Clark, illustrated by Velino Herrera. Copyright 1941 by Ann Nolan Clark, renewed © 1969 by Ann Nolan Clark. *Jenny's Journey* by Sheila White Samton. Copyright © 1991 by Sheila Samton.

Franklin Watts, Inc.: From *North American Indian Sign Language* (Retitled: "Water Signs") by Karen Liptak. Text copyright © 1990 by Karen Liptak.

Albert Whitman & Company: Cover illustration by Irene Trivas from *Not Yet, Yvette* by Helen Ketteman. Illustration © 1992 by Irene Trivas.

Photograph Credits

Key: (t) top, (b) bottom, (c) center.
HBJ/file, 194(t); HBJ/Maria Paraskevas, 194–195

Illustration Credits

Key: (t) top, (b) bottom, (c) center.

Table of Contents Art
Thomas Vroman Associates, Inc., 4, 5, 6, 7

Unit Opener Art
Thomas Vroman Associates, Inc., 8, 9, 112, 113

Bookshelf Art
Thomas Vroman Associates, Inc., 10, 11, 114, 115

Theme Opening Art
Kristen Goeters, 12, 13; Deborah Borgo, 32, 33; Joe Veno, 74, 75, 109

Unit 2
Diane Patterson, 116, 117; Kate Gorman, 136, 137; Carol Nicklaus, 160, 161

Theme Wrap-up Art
Thomas Vroman Associates, Inc., 31, 73, 109, 135, 159, 193

Connection Art
Thomas Vroman Associates, Inc., 110–111; Bill Maughn, 110–111; Kristen Goeters, 195(t)

Selection Art
Marc Brown, 14–25; Scott Scheidly and Ann Morton Hubbard, 26–29; Jose Aruego and Ariane Dewey, 56–70; Sally G. Ward, 76–93; Bernie Knox, 94–96; Floyd Cooper, 97; Maurice Sendak, 98–108; Maryann Kovalski, 118–131; Susanna Natti, 138–146; Velino Herrera, 147; Ben Mahan, 148–157; Arnold Lobel, 162–173; Kid Kane, 174–175; Pat Hutchins, 176–192.